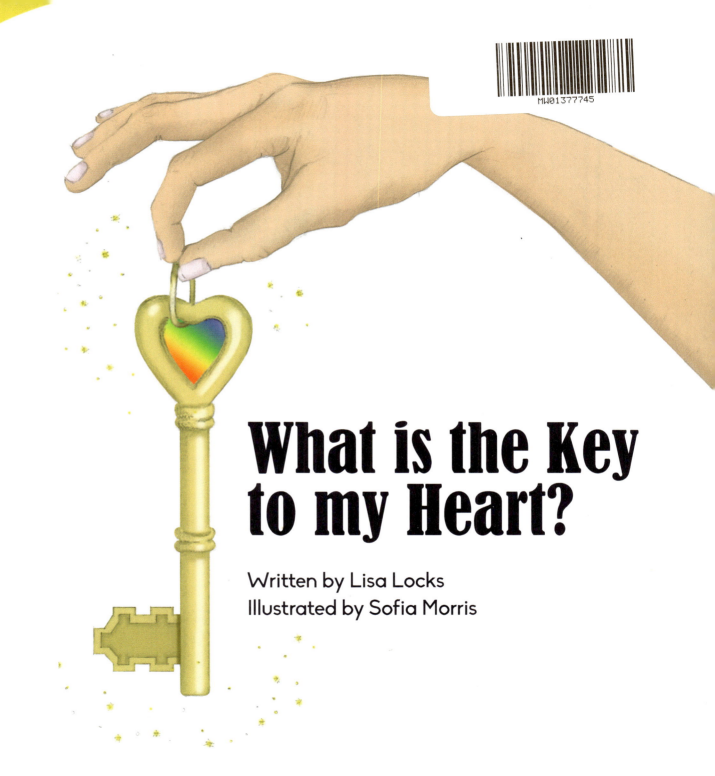

What is the Key to my Heart?

Written by Lisa Locks

Illustrated by Sofia Morris

Published by We Inspire Now Books 2020

Copyright © 2020 Lisa Locks

ISBN
Print: 978-0-6487645-2-6
Hard Copy Print: 978-0-6487645-3-3
Ebook: 978-0-6487645-4-0
All rights are reserved. No part of this publication may be reproduced, stored in or introduced into a retrieval system, or transmitted in any form, or by any means (electronic, mechanical, photocopying, recording or otherwise) without the prior written permission of the author. Any person who does any unauthorised act in relation to this publication may be liable to criminal prosecution and civil claims for damages.
Enquiries should be made through the publisher.

We Inspire Now Books
PO BOX 133 Greensborough,
Victoria Australia 3088
www.weinspirenowbooks.com

Dedication

I lovingly dedicate this book to all the children.
My hope is that my motto becomes yours too.

Being caring and kind is always
on my mind. Helping out a friend
is what is really important
in the end.

Every morning when I wake up
from my beautiful sleep, I tell myself,
'Lisa Locks, this is going to be
an amazing day!'

BELIEVE
believe

I go to my mirror, look
at myself and think what
a beautiful smile.

ENCOURAGE
encourage

I start my day off with a shower.
So then I'm wide awake, alert, and
refreshed for a wonderful day.

I'm looking forward to seeing my friends today!
So I hurry up and get dressed in my school
uniform. Today is going to be fantastic.
I can feel it.

ORGANISE *organise*

Breakfast time! What a great way to start my day with a big bowl of cereal, a glass of juice, and some fruit. Yummy! I'm feeling very satisfied and energised.

I love to have white, clean teeth so I can show my beautiful smile. I brush my teeth up and down, left and right and round and round, making sure they're sparkling clean.

HYGIENE
hygiene

I stand in line with my friend, ready to get on the bus. I ask, 'How are you today?' My friend Casey says, 'Hello, I feel good,' with a big huge smile on her face.

PATIENCE
patience

I'm sitting at my desk in class,
excited to hear what today's lesson
is about. I raise my hand and ask politely,
'What fun things are we learning today?'

POLITE
polite

There goes the bell. It's lunch time and there's a new student in my class. His name is David. I'll take him outside and show him around the school.

CONSIDERATE
considerate

'Catch me if you can!' I call as I run through the school yard past my friend Sofia. 'Tag, you're it,' my friend says, as she catches me.

When the day ends, I get on the bus to go home.
I gaze out the window and picture my future.
I ask myself, 'What I will become – a hairdresser,
an inventor or an author of some kind?'

DREAM
dream

My best friend Zak comes over after school to play. We go outside to play football, and just have some fun.

RELAX
relax

I love to exercise and I choose to
do meditation three times a week.
It makes me feel complete.

It's time to do my homework. I enjoy this time of day because it feels good to complete all of my work and read all types of interesting things.

COMMITTED
committed

Tonight, I have a performance.
I go back to the mirror to find the
confidence within myself to go on stage.
I tell myself it is okay if I don't do as well
as I would like to. I will just do my best.

CONFIDENCE
confidence

I will be the best in all that I do. Once I find the confidence within, happiness will shine through.

I go out on stage and give my best effort. After the show ends, everyone in the audience starts to clap. I feel very proud of myself.

After the show, I go home. It's time to go to sleep. Getting ready for bed, I realise I am happy with how my day went. I'm looking forward to what tomorrow will bring.

HAPPINESS

Happiness

I realise that all the positive things I did were the tools from my personal tool box. I have them all the time with me, inside my heart. I have the key that unlocks them and can unlock them anytime I want. With a smile on my face, I close my eyes and go to sleep.

My Tool Box *and the key*

My Heart

My Magical Tool Box is the key to my heart. It unlocks and creates words to help me love myself and others. Happiness is within my heart.

My Key

Questions
Questions
?

- What positive things could happen today?
- What can you do to encourage yourself?
- What exciting things do you dream you will become?
- What do you need to do to be organised?
- What can you do to have good hygiene?
- What could you do to be considerate to others?
- What exciting adventures do you do for fun?
- What does happiness mean to you?

Biography

Lisa Locks is a mother of two beautiful adult children and mother to their partners and their dogs. Lisa also shares her house with many international students of different nationalities and borders and runs her own hairdressing business from home. There is never a dull moment in her house since there are a lot of people coming in and out every day.

Lisa has always been in tune with her children and others. The realisation of how much love she has for children has inspired her to write children's books. Lisa understands that every child is different and therefore believes that it is important to provide good, fundamental guidelines, and for each child to know that loving themselves is the key. Once they know that, everything else falls into place.

Through the years of hardship of being divorced, raising her two children, dealing with the constant juggling act of work, school-runs and sports activities that has kept her busy, Lisa has been able to grow as a person and gradually come to understand how to love herself with all her flaws.

She has learnt to love and accept herself and become aware and take responsibility for her own decisions. Lisa's positive attitude and her own belief system, which she calls her key, underpins her ongoing motivation and commitment and allows her to reach for her dreams and goals.

Lisa's determination, even her little feistiness and frustrations, keeps her passion alive which allows her to love and enjoy every minute that she lives. Lisa aims to, 'Live in my thoughts, my feelings and my behaviour - my words are my world.' With this powerful message, Lisa aspires to spread a positive energy wherever she goes, thereby shaping the future generations.

Her motto is:

Being caring and kind is always on my mind. Helping out a friend is what is really important in the end.

www.lisaslocks.com

Acknowledgements

I would love to SHOUT OUT a thank you to each and every beautiful human being, who has been involved in sharing with me my dreams and making them come true.

Now I am a Author. WOW - WHAT IS THE KEY TO MY HEART? BY LISA LOCKS

Firstly a big thank you to:

The adorable and kind-hearted Sofia Morris for being my illustrator and my beautiful friend; she takes pride in her work as you can see in her illustrations.

Charlene for being my go-between and putting up with my craziness - another friend who is kindhearted and very lovable.

Chantelle my incredible, kind and yet always inspiring friend who always brought me back to my original vision. One would say she put me back on track.

Kellie, who was the one who showed me how to be organised and I will always love her for that.

Adam, what can I say about this amazing musician? I have known him since we were teenagers - he is a beautiful soul. We have a song coming out soon representing the book. I'm so excited. Thank you Adam.

My friends and family and you know who you are - what would I do without your support? I will be forever grateful and love you always.

Lucky last Antoinette Pellegrini, my publisher. Well where do I start? When I first met Antoinette I was like a puppy dog and followed her every where until I caught her attention and from then on we have become friends. Antoinette has given me the strength to believe in myself to make me proud to be the author I am today. I will always be grateful that she came into my life when it was time.

I now believe I can make any of my dreams come true.

CPSIA information can be obtained at www.ICGtesting.com
Printed in the USA
LVIW010008100920
664724LV00002B/11